Would You Rather...
SHAKE like a
DOG or CLIMB
like a CAT?

Camilla de la Bédoyère and Mel Howells

Would you rather...

shake like a dog,

climb like a cat,

jump like a rabbit,

or burrow like a gerbil?

You'll be dry in no time!

A dog has loose skin so it can really shake! When it's wet, it shakes to remove the water from its fur – it only takes four seconds! In the wild, it's important for a dog to get dry quickly otherwise it might get cold and sick.

You'd be great at climbing but careful you don't get stuck.

Cats can jump seven times their own height and zoom up a tree at lightning speed to escape from danger. But the curved shape of their claws makes it tricky for them to get down so fast – or at all!

You'd be super at karate kicks if you could jump like a rabbit!

Bouncing bunnies love to jump, leap, twist and kick. But their joyful dancing isn't just for fun - wild rabbits jump to escape the jaws of hungry foxes. Their long, strong legs can deliver a mighty kick too!

If you could burrow like a gerbil, you'd be able to dig an amazing underground home.

Gerbils live in burrows with their families in hot, dry places. They only come out at night when it is cooler. They dig tunnels up to three metres long and build nests in them. They keep stores of food underground too.

Would you rather...

picnic with
a rat,

grab a snack
with a snake,

lunch with
a guinea pig,

or nibble with
a hen?

If you shared a picnic with a rat, you'd have to eat a lot of rotting rubbish!

A rat might pack some delicious snacks like cake and sandwiches but keep an eye out for stinky surprises. Wild rats eat anything, including rotting plants and other animals. They even eat other rats!

Lip-smacking snakes love huge snacks! But you'd have to stretch to fit it all in.

Snakes can't chew their food so it all goes down in one great gulp. Some snakes eat animals bigger than themselves, and a massive meal might last them for weeks.

You might regret having lunch with a guinea pig!

Guinea pigs eat their own droppings. They nibble grass and other tough plants that are hard to digest, so they eat the poo again to help them get even more goodness from their food.

If you nibbled with a hen, you'd have to spend all day eating wriggly worms!

In the wild, hens spend hours pecking at bugs, worms and seeds on the ground. You'd have to spend all day eating, and you still might feel a little peckish!

Would you rather...

have a mouse
for a mum,

a tortoise
for a dad,

a hamster
for a sister,

or a tarantula
for a brother?

If your mum was a mouse, she'd carry you in her mouth – by the scruff of your neck!

Mice are good, caring mothers. They look after their babies, feeding them and licking them clean. But if a mouse baby goes off to explore, its mum will carry it back to the nest using her teeth!

A tortoise would be a boring, snoring dad.

Some tortoises sleep for up to six months at a time. If the weather is cold and there isn't much food, they'd rather spend the chilly winter snoozing (hibernating).

Beware – your hamster sister might steal your treats!

Hamsters have huge cheek pouches to fill with their favourite treats. The pouches are like bags of skin. There's no spit in the pouches so the food stays dry and they can carry it home to eat later.

You'd have to keep your brother happy, or he might give you the most terrible itch.

This grumpy tarantula fires itchy hairs from his body when he's scared or angry. He has got eight legs and can run pretty fast, so he's bound to catch you if you tried to run away.

Would you rather talk with...

a dog,

a cat,

a horse,

or a chameleon?

You would have to like the smell of wee!

Dogs use their barks and their bottoms to talk to each other. A dog can learn a lot about another dog from the stink of its wee and how its bottom smells – that's why they have some of the best noses in the animal world.

You'd have to get really close to talk to a kitty.

A cat likes to rub its cheeks against you to leave its smell. Cats like their owners to smell just like them! When a cat purrs it's showing you it is happy.

You'd need big ears and a long nose to speak with a horse.

A horse moves its ears around to show how it is feeling.
If it's nervous, its ears go back and it might snort to
warn other horses of danger.

But, sometimes, a snort just means
that a horse's huge nose is full of snot
and it's about to blow... yuk!

You'd have to change colour
to chat with a chameleon!

A boy panther chameleon is
normally blue or green but
when it gets angry or feels
threatened, his skin turns red
to warn other chameleons that
they should stay away.

Would you rather...

have eyes like a goldfish,

teeth like a chinchilla,

skin like an iguana,

or legs like a hamster?

If you had eyes like a goldfish, you'd have super sight!

Goldfish live in ponds, where the water is often muddy and murky. They have a great sense of smell, big eyes and special night vision to help them find their prey in the dark.

You would have to brush your teeth a lot if they were like a chinchilla's - they'd be huge!

A chinchilla's teeth are orange-yellow and can grow five centimetres in just one year. A chinchilla eats tough grasses and seeds which quickly wears away their teeth - that's why they need teeth that keep growing.

It wouldn't be great having skin like an iguana – it would keep peeling off!

Humans lose tiny flakes of skin every minute, but iguanas can lose a whole layer of scaly skin at a time! It's called moulting, and iguanas moult when they have grown too big for the skin they're in. Some iguanas can grow up to five or six feet – about the size of an adult human. That's a lot of new skin to grow!

If you had legs like a hamster, you'd win a gold medal for running!

A hamster's legs may look small and thin, but they are fantastic runners! These furry little animals need to run so they can escape from other animals, but pet hamsters always like to be prepared and love to keep fit by running on their wheels.

Pet Awards!

Which pet would you rather be?

The Furriest Pet

Chinchilla fur is the softest and furriest in the world. They have to bathe in dust or volcanic ash to keep it clean.

Chinchilla

The Friendliest Pet

Most pets are friendly but horses win this award. They live in groups, called herds, and they love company.

Horse

The Smoothest Pet

If you stroke a pet snake, you will discover that the scales on its skin are cool, smooth and silky.

Snake

The Noisiest Pet

Cats purr to show they are feeling happy, sad or are in pain. The big cats, such as lions and tigers, roar but they can't purr.

Cat

Tortoise

The Slowest Pet

A human walks about 2.5 times faster than a tortoise. If a tortoise is scared, it hides in its shell instead of running away.

The Squeakiest Pet

Mice make quiet squeaks. We can't even hear all of the sounds they make. But guinea pig squeaks can be very loud! They sound like 'wheek-wheek'.

Guinea pig

More Pet Fun!

Stay safe and ask a grown-up to help you.

Sniff and smell

Dogs have a great sense of smell. How good is your sense of smell? Choose smelly things, such as cheese, soap and dirty socks. Blindfold a friend and challenge them to identify each smelly thing, without peeking or touching!

Would you rather...?

Think of some 'Would you rather...?' questions to share with your friends or family. Visit your local library and research different pets to create your own fun questions.

Investigate!

Choose your favourite type of pet and find out how you would look after it. Where would your pet sleep, what would it eat and what would you need to do to take care of it? Draw a picture of your special pet and give it a name.

Be a bunny!

Use card to make a strip that fits around your head. Cut out some paper bunny ears and attach them to the card. You can use coloured pens or stickers to decorate your bunny ears.

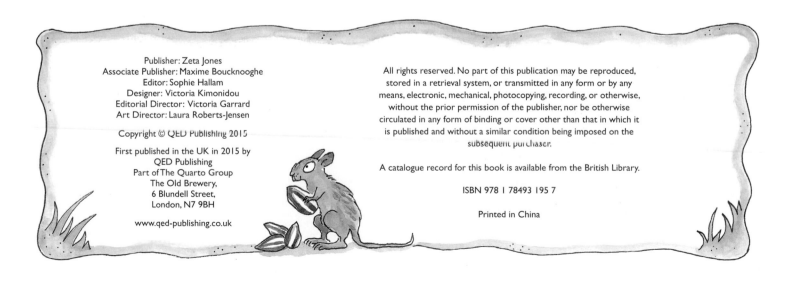

Publisher: Zeta Jones
Associate Publisher: Maxime Boucknooghe
Editor: Sophie Hallam
Designer: Victoria Kimonidou
Editorial Director: Victoria Garrard
Art Director: Laura Roberts-Jensen

Copyright © QED Publishing 2015

First published in the UK in 2015 by
QED Publishing
Part of The Quarto Group
The Old Brewery,
6 Blundell Street,
London, N7 9BH

www.qed-publishing.co.uk

A catalogue record for this book is available from the British Library.

ISBN 978 1 78493 195 7

Printed in China